Perfectly Hidden

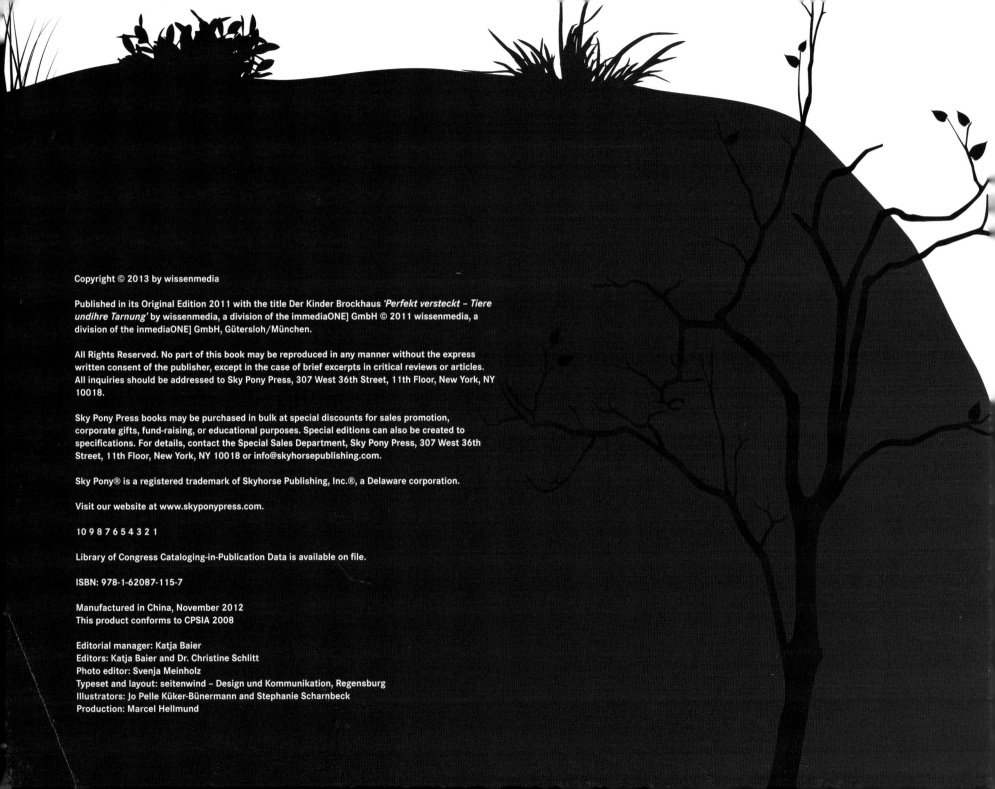

Sky Pony Press books may be purchased in bulk at special discounts for sales promotion, corporate gifts, fund-raising, or educational purposes. Special editions can also be created to specifications. For details, contact the Special Sales Department, Sky Pony Press, 307 West 36th Street, 11th Floor, New York, NY 10018 or info@skyhorsepublishing.com.

Sky Pony® is a registered trademark of Skyhorse Publishing, Inc.®, a Delaware corporation.

Visit our website at www.skyponypress.com.

10 9 8 7 6 5 4 3 2 1

Library of Congress Cataloging-in-Publication Data is available on file.

ISBN: 978-1-62087-115-7

Manufactured in China, November 2012
This product conforms to CPSIA 2008

Editorial manager: Katja Baier
Editors: Katja Baier and Dr. Christine Schlitt
Photo editor: Svenja Meinholz
Typeset and layout: seitenwind – Design und Kommunikation, Regensburg
Illustrators: Jo Pelle Küker-Bünermann and Stephanie Scharnbeck
Production: Marcel Hellmund

Perfectly Hidden

The Animal Kingdom's Fascinating Camouflage

Christine Schlitt
Translated by Chris Brandt

Sky Pony Press
New York

Contents

Insects

Spiders

Crustaceans

Mollusks

Jellyfish

Hello, our names are Maya and Karl Clever,
and we'll go with you through this book.

Fish

Birds

Amphibians

Mammals

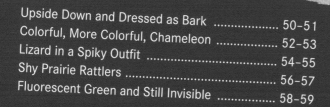

Reptiles

Perfectly Hidden Is Halfway to Survival!

Why do polar bears have white fur? Why do zebras have stripes? Why do some grasshoppers look like orchids, twigs, or leaves? Why are rays flat and jellyfish transparent? And why do some fish look like rocks? The answer to all these questions: for survival! Camouflaging themselves so they can be as unnoticeable as possible, or so they can look like a completely different animal to their enemies, is just as common for most animals as propagating their species and eating. Good camouflage helps keep them from being eaten. Animals also use their camouflage in order to ambush their prey effectively. Most species have developed clever techniques as they have evolved over millions of years, so they can—by being perfectly hidden—make themselves almost invisible in their habitats.

Tactic Number One: I make myself invisible! Animals that use this tactic fit perfectly into their surroundings with the shape of their bodies, the coloring of their skin or their feathers, and their behavior. They look like blossoms, twigs, tree bark, leaves swaying in the breeze, algae, stones, or the sea floor. The flat-tailed gecko (photo) for example, which lives in Madagascar, imitates the wrinkled leaves of its habitat so perfectly that it is almost completely invisible to its possible predators. Researchers call this sort of camouflage "mimesis." The animals that use it want their camouflage to fool their enemies into thinking they are lifeless and completely uninteresting as something to eat.

Tactic Number Two: I will make myself look unappetizing! Bright coloring like the wasp's yellow-and-black stripes or the red-and-black rings around the coral snake are signals to other animals: Watch out! I am dangerous or bad-tasting! Predators keep a distance between themselves and these well-defended animals. But not every animal that sports this sort of color warning is truly dangerous. Some completely harmless animals make use of their relatives' bad reputations and wear the same colors to scare off predators. The coloring of the bad-tasting Monarch butterfly (above left), for example, is imitated by the female of the species with the scientific name *Hypolimnas misippus* (left). Researchers call this kind of hiding tactic "mimicry."

Tactic Number Three: I make myself invisible so I can ambush my prey better! Many predators, like the polar bear (above right) or the leopard, use the inconspicuous coloring of their coats in order to sneak up on their prey unnoticed and attack from very close range. But the trick of coat color is still very simple. Many animals have developed even more subtle tricks of camouflage in the course of their evolution to lure their prey into their traps. The carpet crocodile fish (*Papilloculiceps longiceps*, photo below right), for example, can hardly be distinguished from the ocean floor as it waits patiently for its prey to swim past. The frogfish even puts out bait in order to lure its prey.

Invisible Among the Leaves

It hangs from a tree, it's flat and mostly green, and it sways softly in the breeze. Do you think it's a leaf? That only might be true, because it could also be a walking leaf. These insects, which live in Southeast Asia, look remarkably like the leaves of a tree. They live in trees and eat leaves whose shapes and colors they imitate down to the smallest details. Even withered and somewhat ragged leaf-edges are part of their camouflage. But they imitate not only the leaves' shape and color, but also their movements. When a breeze blows through the actual leaves, they begin to sway back and forth like a real leaf. That's how they pretend to their predators not to be interesting prey.

Walking leaves

"Mimesis" is what biologists call the animals' trick of imitating the shapes of plants or even other animals, thereby making themselves optically indistinguishable from their surroundings in order to fool predators. Walking leaves are not the only ones who use this method; many other animals and plants do, too, including the stick insects.

Male walking leaves are often in short supply. Sometimes there is only one male for 500 females. That's why the females can have babies without the males.

The great walking leaf of Thailand grows to a length of over 4 inches (10 centimeters). It is the largest of the walking leaves.

When the walking leaves come out of the egg, they look like brown ants. That way they are well camouflaged on the ground. As soon as they find a plant, they crawl up it and turn into "living" leaves.

Unique deception: The walking leaf's body and wings are flattened like leaves and its legs appear as new growth. The females produce chirping sounds with their antenna.

Walking leaves live on trees and bushes in tropical Southeast Asia. During the day they hang motionless among the leaves and only with the coming of darkness do they begin looking for food.

Leaf? Or maybe it is an insect? With extremely flat bodies sprinkled with yellow-green coloring, wings and legs that look like half-eaten leaves, and veins that look just like a leaf, the walking leaves are hard to tell apart from their environment.

Rainforest Ghosts

You could stand right next to a walking stick and still not see it. It has a long, skinny, dry body and thin legs, and it hangs motionless on shrubs so it's hard to tell it apart from the shrubs' actual twigs. Camouflaged like this, it protects itself perfectly from its predators, who take it for just another dry twig and ignore it in their hunt for food. These insects, whose home is in the tropics and subtropics, hang stiffly amid the branches even when they feel threatened, since the moment they try to flee, their camouflage is gone.

Walking sticks

Typically, insects have fore and rear wings, but in most stick insects these have atrophied. Still, there are some kinds with well-developed and even colorful wings.

Like the wandering leaves, the stick insects belong among the ghost insects. Their scientific name is phasmatodea, from the Greek word phasma, meaning "ghost." They are called ghosts because their camouflage makes them invisible, like ghosts and phantoms.

Adult walking sticks live their entire lives among the twigs of shrubs and bushes. During the day they rest and only wake with the coming of dusk, when most of their natural enemies, like birds and lizards, are asleep.

Female walking sticks, like the female walking leaves, need no males in order to have babies! With their so-called "virgin births," their offspring develop in eggs that have not been fertilized. However, such "virgin births" produce almost no males.

Most walking sticks can neither fly nor make big jumps like their distant grasshopper relatives. They just walk very slowly through the branches.

The walking sticks grow to be the longest insects in the world. The bodies of the genus *Acrophylla* can reach a length of over 8 inches (20 centimeters)! So, some of these are also known as "walking branches."

If you look very closely, only then can you tell the walking stick apart from the twigs it's standing on. The thin, brown-gray bodies and the long skinny legs are perfect imitations of the shrub's twigs!

Predatory Orchid Imitators

The orchid mantis (*Hymenopus coronatus*) has its hunting grounds among the leaves and blossoms of tropical plants. There, it waits for its prey. This predatory insect-eater likes to live among orchids. When a careless insect comes looking for the nectar of the lovely flower, the hunter's strong forearms reach forward like jackknives and grab the surprised prey. Even well-defended insects like wasps or bees are usually no match for the powerful forearms. Helpless in its struggle to survive, the prey is then torn apart and eaten alive by the orchid mantis's powerful jaws.

Orchid mantises

The orchid mantis does not need to drink any water; it gets enough liquid from its food.

The orchid mantis has a small black dot on its back, which can confuse a small fly. The fly thinks the unremarkable spot is another little fly and lands next to it. This, in turn, lures larger flies, which are one of the favorite items in an orchid mantis's diet.

The orchid mantis sits perfectly motionless in its blossom, waiting for its prey. However, should the prey land too far away, the hunter-insect see-saws back and forth as it moves, like a blossom blown by the wind, so it can slowly get close enough to its unsuspecting prey without being noticed.

Orchid mantises are usually white, but there are some with pink, red, greenish, and even brownish coloring. The forearms spread apart to imitate the appearance of orchid blossoms and they give the mantis perfect camouflage.

The orchid mantis gets its name from its surroundings. It likes to live mostly in the damp tropical and subtropical rainforests of Southeast Asia.

Because of its white coloring and its spread forelegs, the orchid mantis blends almost completely into its environment. Perfectly camouflaged and hoping that a careless insect will come close, the predator insect sits completely motionless for long periods on the orchid's petals.

The Peppered Moth's Trick

The peppered moth is a butterfly that's very common in northern latitudes. Have you ever seen one in the woods or in a garden? No wonder! Like almost no other butterfly, the unremarkable peppered moth, in its camouflage costume, fits perfectly into its surroundings. During the days, this moth rests on the branches or trunks of trees and becomes active only with the coming of dusk. To protect itself from its predators, its white wings are peppered with many black spots. On birch bark this wing pattern makes the moth as good as invisible. And on the bark of other trees, it cleverly fools birds by appearing to be a dry and tasteless spot.

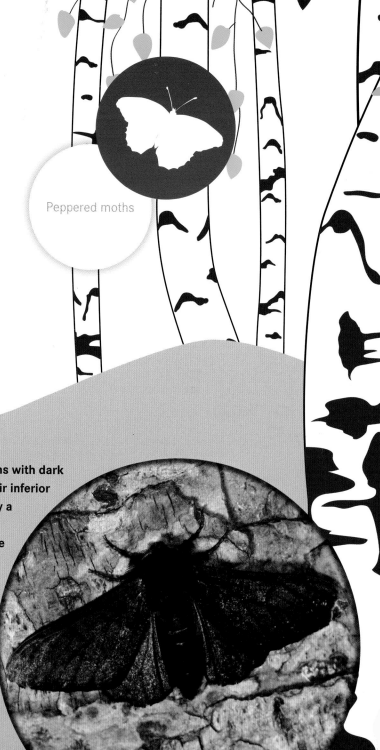

Peppered moths

The peppered moth belongs to the largest family of butterflies, with about 26,000 kinds worldwide.

Many relatives of the peppered moth sport a kind of camouflage that makes them almost invisible on tree bark—for example, the willow beauty and the orange moth.

The peppered moth lives in open forests, meadows, gardens, and parks in Central Europe, North America, and Asia.

There are also peppered moths with dark wing markings. Normally, their inferior camouflage gives them hardly a chance to survive in nature. However, in areas where there is a lot of pollution where soot leaves a coating of black on the bark of the trees, they have the advantage and increase more readily than their white relatives.

Blackbirds, thrushes, yellowhammers, and robins have a hard time finding the peppered moth on tree bark. The clever night moth doesn't rely on its coloring alone, though; it also chooses its resting place carefully. Usually it perches on the underside of a branch or in a shadowy place.

With a wingspan of up to 2⅓ inches (6 centimeters), the peppered moth is one of the largest of the European butterflies.

Walking Twigs

You can recognize inchworms, or spanworms, immediately by the peculiar way they move. The larvae of these worms, which belong to the same butterfly family as the peppered moth, push their hindquarters up very close to their heads, so their bodies bend upward like a clothespin. Then, they stretch their heads as far forward as they can. But even though they propel themselves in such a noticeable way, inchworms are masters of camouflage. Their long thin bodies are colored exactly like the twigs of the trees where they live and where they devour many, many leaves. When they use their pairs of forefeet to climb onto a branch and then stretch their bodies straight out from the branch, you can hardly tell them apart from the other surrounding twigs.

Inchworms

Forest rangers and gardeners do not like inchworms at all. The worms like to eat tender buds and leaves and therefore damage many trees. Sometimes they can even strip a tree of leaves completely.

Did you know that butterflies spend most of their lives as worms? They spend only a few weeks, sometimes only days, fluttering through woods, gardens, parks, and meadows as brightly colored aerial acrobats.

This worm spends its life doing nothing but eating. As it grows, it has to shed its skin, because the skin does not grow along with the worm. As it molts for the last time, it changes into a pupa or chrysalis, from which a butterfly will emerge.

Inchworms feed on juicy leaves. You can find them from April through August, often on oaks, birches, poplars, and willows, but also on rosebushes and raspberry and currant bushes. Try to find these camouflage artists some time!

An elegant worm-step along a branch: When the inchworm pushes its hindquarters up close to its head with its two pair of rear feet, its back bends up like a cat's.

Can you find the inchworm? Hardly any other insects can make themselves so invisible. For not only do the worms imitate the color and shape of small branches perfectly, but sometimes they even have what seems to be little leaf buds on their bodies. For the inchworms this is absolutely a matter of life and death, because they are the favorite food of many kinds of birds!

The Magical Transformation of the Oakleaf Butterflies

Butterflies are among the most colorful insects on earth. Their wings shimmer with numerous bright colors. The Oakleaf butterflies, which live in Southeast Asia and Australia, sport notably colorful decorations. However, they are noticeable only while flying. As soon as an Oakleaf butterfly lands on a branch, it closes its wings together tightly. And then an amazing thing happens: The butterfly is suddenly invisible! Is it magic? No, it's merely a perfect mimesis. The undersides of the Oakleaf butterfly's wings are deceptively realistic copies of dry, withered leaves.

Oakleaf butterflies

With their wingspans of 3 ½ to 4 ¾ inches (9 to 12 centimeters), the tropical Oakleaf butterflies are bigger than most species we are familiar with.

Oakleaf butterflies live in the thick tropical forests of India, Myanmar, Thailand, Southern China, and Australia.

The scientific name for the Oakleaf butterfly is kallima. This genus name is derived from the Greek word kalós, for "beautiful."

The bright colors on the top of the wings give no hint to how cleverly the Indian Oakleaf butterfly pulls the wool over its predators' eyes when its wings are closed.

The Indian Oakleaf butterfly takes no chances with its camouflage: Little dark sprinkles on the undersides of its wings imitate mold growth, and gray spots imitate the lichen on the leaf it pretends to be.

Which leaf is the butterfly? The gray-brown wings of the Oakleaf butterfly look almost exactly like a withered leaf. They not only imitate its shape and coloring perfectly, but the thin dark lines look just like the veins of a leaf, and the little tail on each of the rear wings looks like a leaf stem. The Oakleaf butterfly simply touches a branch with its tail and presto, the leaf "grows" right out of the branch.

Look Out, It's Spiny!

Treehoppers look like insects from another planet. Strange stud-like growths reach up into the air from its protective exterior. Some of these have weird outgrowths that look like antennas. Others have four hairy black balls on a stalk, which allow these insects to detect the air currents caused by approaching enemies. Although many tree-hoppers sport such an eccentric appearance, many others are real camouflage artists. The buffalo treehopper, which is found in Europe, can hardly be distinguished from a bright green leaf. And the carapace of the treehopper known as *Umbonia crassicornis* looks deceptively like a real thorn.

Treehoppers

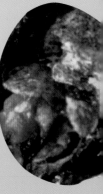

The thorny treehopper, native to Germany, camouflages itself cleverly with two defensive protrusions on its back that look like thorns—the ideal costume for sitting unnoticed on a blackberry branch.

Sometimes ants and treehoppers strike up a special friendship. Some ants love the sugary mud that treehoppers exude. They drink it and in return protect the treehoppers sitting on the branches.

Imitating the look of thorns on a rosebush, the treehopper sits motionless in its natural environment. But if a hungry predator should come close, it disappears with one powerful hop out of the enemy's field of vision.

The buffalo treehopper is not actually native to Europe. It originally came from North America. It traveled to Europe around a hundred years ago on the branches of little fruit trees and made itself at home. Animals that have come to a new region because of humans are called "alien" or non-native species.

Most kinds of treehoppers are native to the tropics. There are over 250 species in North America. Some of these are feared by orchard farmers and vintners, since they can use their proboscises to cut into leaves and twigs and then suck out sap; they can damage the wood so much this way that the parts of the plant they've affected die off.

The littlest treehoppers grow to only around 4 ½ millimeters. The biggest, to which the Hemikyptha also belongs, can be as long as 1 inch (2 ½ centimeters).

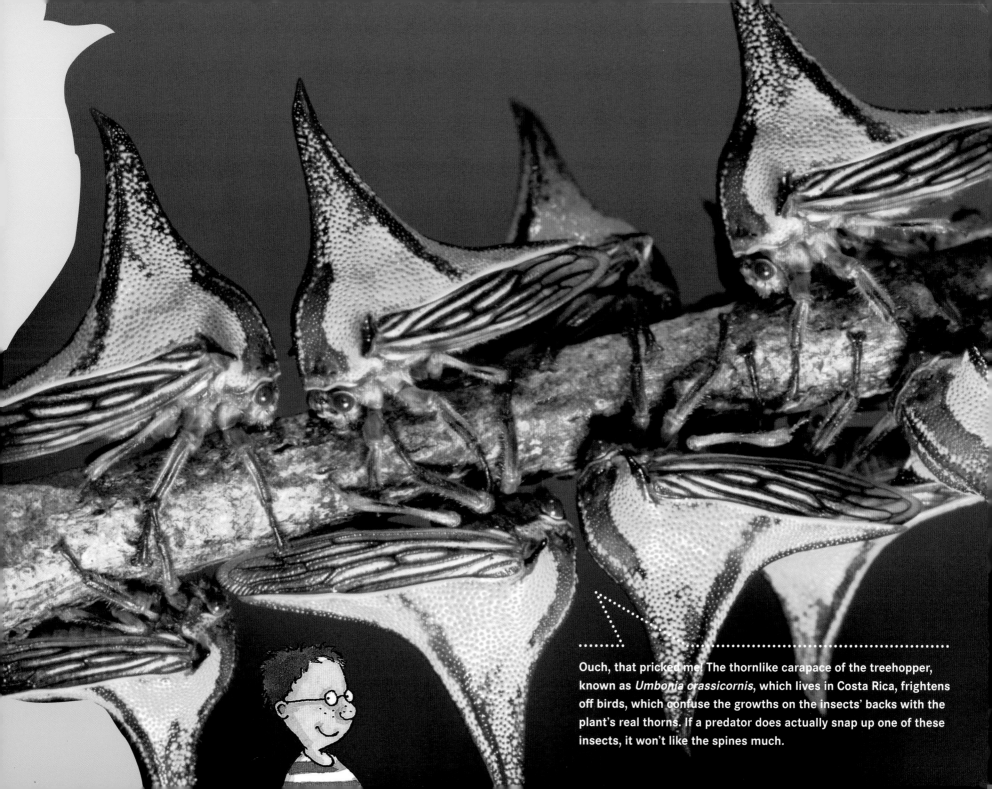

Ouch, that pricked me! The thornlike carapace of the treehopper, known as *Umbonia crassicornis*, which lives in Costa Rica, frightens off birds, which confuse the growths on the insects' backs with the plant's real thorns. If a predator does actually snap up one of these insects, it won't like the spines much.

What's Painting Itself with Someone Else's Stripes?

Why hide if you can fool predators in a much more cunning way? That must be what the hoverflies think. The bodies of these harmless insects, who nourish themselves on flower nectar, are covered with conspicuous black-and-yellow stripes. This is a signal in the animal world that means *look out, I'm dangerous!* Birds, for example, know that hunting wasps will not agree with them, since the wasps' stingers are very painful. The hoverflies use such fear to their advantage; they imitate the black-and-yellow coloring of wasps, bees, and hornets to scare off their predators.

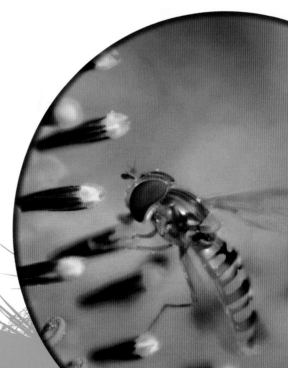

Scientists call this popular method of imitating the coloring or shape of foul-tasting or poisonous relatives to protect oneself from predators "mimicry."

Hoverflies

Hoverflies are real aerial acrobats. They can fly sideways and backwards and even hang in the air like a helicopter. This "hovering" in the air is what gives them their name.

One kind of hoverfly, which imitates the appearance of the honeybee, lays its eggs in cesspools. That's why it's often called a manure bee. The manure bee's larvae breathe through a long, thin breathing tube—a kind of snorkel—which is attached to the rear of their bodies.

Hoverflies are very useful insects. As they fly from blossom to blossom to drink nectar, they also pollinate the flowers.

The real thing or a fake? The black-and-yellow warning colors worn by the hoverfly look deceptively genuine. The bright stripes on the hind part of its body signal to predators, *watch out, I sting!* And the hoverfly has thoroughly tricked any animal that believes it actually does.

Invisible in a Sea of Blossoms

Why build a web when your prey passes right in front of your jaws? That's what the crab spiders must think. Perfectly hidden, they lurk in white or yellow flowers, patiently waiting for their prey. The insects hurrying past usually have little chance to recognize this master of camouflage in time. As long as the crab spider sits on flower petals of its own color without moving, it is very hard to recognize. Some of these eight-legged flower-dwellers can even change their colors, so one that's a pristine white with red stripes can quickly become a bright yellow golden-rod spider.

Crab spiders

Besides the white and yellow crab spiders who live on blossoms, there are also green ones who live on leaves and brown ones whose home is on tree trunks or close to the earth.

Crab spiders are only about 1 centimeter long on average. But that does not keep them from overpowering remarkably large and well-defended insects. Among their favorite foods, for example, are honey bees.

Some crab spiders plan ahead. After they capture their prey they wrap it with a silken thread into a handy package and stow it under the blossom where they live.

Crab spiders are homebodies. Often a crab spider will spend almost its entire life on one and the same plant, for example on a grass tree.

These spiders are called crab spiders thanks to their extremely long foreleg pairs. The forelegs sit at a slight angle when the spider is at rest, giving the spider the appearance of a crab with large pincers. And what's more: with their side legs they can move sideways like crabs.

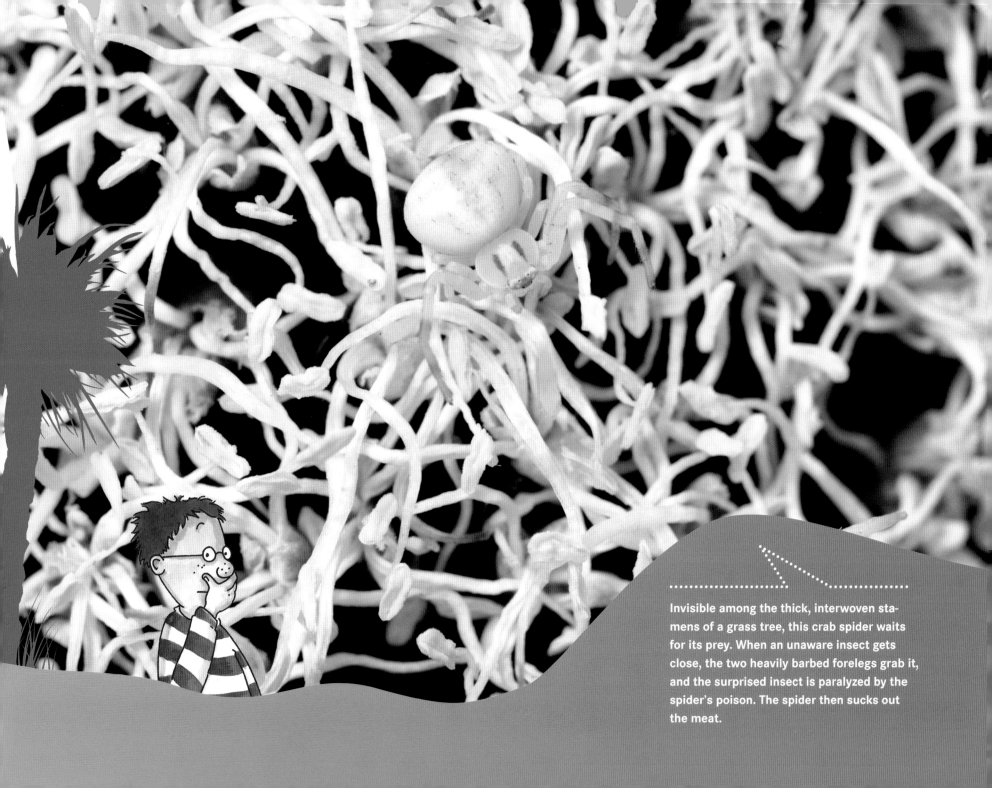

Invisible among the thick, interwoven stamens of a grass tree, this crab spider waits for its prey. When an unaware insect gets close, the two heavily barbed forelegs grab it, and the surprised insect is paralyzed by the spider's poison. The spider then sucks out the meat.

Crabs with Roof Gardens

Camouflage the pattern of your skin, grow a crusty shell that looks like stone, or change your skin color—anyone can do that sort of thing! Or so the spider crabs must think. These little crabs, who live in the ocean, have figured out one of the strangest camouflages in the animal kingdom. They decorate their triangular back shells and their legs with all sorts of stuff that they collect on their walks across the rocky ocean bottoms: mussel shells, algae, seaweeds, anemones, or little sponges. These creative crabs with roof gardens on their backs are therefore known as decorator crabs.

Spider crabs cannot swim. They creep across the ocean floor with their long legs. Whatever appears right in front of their powerful pincer arms they either eat or collect as decorating material.

Decorator crabs

The decorator crab, with its two long pincer arms, snaps up its materials from its surroundings and fastens them to hook-like brushes—a sort of Velcro—that covers its shell and legs.

The biggest spider crabs on earth are related to the little decorator crab. The body of the Japanese giant crab grows to about 17 ½ inches (45 centimeters) long, and its legs have a span of more than 10 feet (3 meters)!

Spider crabs are not spiders! These ten-legged crabs got that name because of their long legs, which look like spider legs.

What happens to the shell's décor when the designer crab grows and sheds its skin? The environmentally conscious spider crab does not just throw away the old shell's camouflage; it reuses it. It carefully cuts the laboriously collected decorative material off the old shell with its pincers and puts it on the hardened new shell. Perfect recycling!

Underneath the algae, anemones, little pieces of sponge, and seaweed on its protective shell, the spider crab is hardly recognizable. The algae and the anemones are also food for the spider crab—how practical! When there is no snack close enough to catch, the hungry omnivore can make a meal from its own roof garden.

Well Camouflaged in the Mud Flats

In the summer walking across tidal flats, such as those of the North Sea, have you ever seen a prawn burrowed into the sand? You have to look carefully to discover this swimming crayfish, which is about 3 inches (8 centimeters) long. Its speckled shell matches the sandy subsoil perfectly. But the North Sea prawns, for example, are masters of disguise in the ocean as well. These thieves, active at night, stay in deeper waters during the day. There everything looks blue, because the water 165 feet (50 meters) deep or more lets in only the wavelength of blue light. The sly prawn makes itself invisible by putting on its blue camouflage coloring. At night, when it comes up to the water surface to hunt for its prey, it changes its color from sandy to blue-green.

North Sea prawns

North Sea prawns are often called "crabs." Even so, the prawns are not crabs at all. Crabs are roundish with tough shells and powerful pincers, and they walk sideways. The prawns, in contrast, have long bodies and feelers.

As the young prawns grow they must molt, since their leathery shells do not grow along with them. After they've molted, the prawns must be especially careful of predators, since it takes some time until the new shell hardens into a good defense.

Only about one in 50,000 prawn eggs grows into an adult prawn. The rest are eaten or die in some other way.

North Sea prawns live on algae, tiny crabs, and worms. But they also nibble at feet now and then. As you wander across the tidal flats, stick your foot into a tidal inlet. Perhaps you will soon notice that a hungry prawn has mistaken your foot for delicious prey.

The night-hunting prawns locate their prey by their sense of smell. Their eyes are not made for the hunt, as they can only distinguish between light and dark.

During the fall and winter seasons, prawns live in the deeper parts of the ocean, which do not cool as much as the more shallow waters. In summer, prawns wander into the warmer tidal flats. There you can find them burrowed into the sand.

When prawns burrow down into the sand of the tidal flats on summer days, they can hardly be distinguished from the grains of sand. They only come into the flats with high tide, and during the ebb tide they often stay in tidal pools or inlets.

Phantoms of the Deep

Cephalopods are the most inventive camouflage artists and tricksters of all the animals. Some of these intelligent ocean dwellers, including octopuses, squids, and cuttlefish, use several different techniques at the same time to fool their enemies. Everyone knows that these "inkfish" squirt out a cloud of black liquid when they sense danger and duck behind the dark cloud to disappear. But did you know that these cephalopods (literally, "head-feet" animals) can also change the colors, patterns, and surface structure of their skins in a matter of seconds in order to match their background?

Cephalopods

Even their popular name leads us astray: "Inkfish" are namely not fish at all. Rather, they belong to the mollusk family, like mussels and snails. They have no skeleton, and most of them have no hard external shell. (The exception is the nautilus.)

Cephalopods belong to the oldest known animals on earth. They have populated our planet for 500 million years.

You can tell cephalopods apart by the number of their arms: octopuses have eight arms; cuttlefish and giant squid have eight arms plus two tentacles, equaling ten. Since the arms grow directly out of the head, these animals are called "cephalopods" from the Greek meaning "head-foot."

One of the most sophisticated camouflage methods is employed by the dwarf Hawaiian bobtail squid, with the scientific name Euprymna scolopes. When it goes hunting by moonlight in shallow waters, this creature runs the danger of becoming a meal for predatory fish—these predators hunt prey that mostly swims above them. Therefore Euprymna scolopes sends out light with the aid of phosphorescent bacteria. That way the outline of its body, seen from below, dissolves into the moonlight, and the hunters below cannot see it.

When they are in danger, cephalopods squirt out a dark cloud of black ink. That's how they mislead their enemies and can slip off into the distance without being seen. The ink is composed of the pigment melanin, which is the source of dark skin color among humans. In Italian cuisine the ink is also used to make black noodles.

Master changeling: A cephalopod's skin is studded with pigment cells, the so-called chromatophores. These cells can be turned on and off by tiny muscles to change the animal's appearance—up to a thousand times a day!

Quick-change Artists with Eight Arms

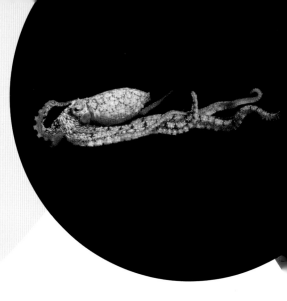

When divers first observed the mimic octopus in action, they couldn't believe their eyes. As danger approached, this octopus, with its pattern of white-and-black stripes, suddenly turned into a puffed-up sea-spider, only to swim away a moment later disguised as a flounder with its legs pressed close together. The researchers wondered: Was this octopus imitating the appearance and behavior of other animals? In fact they found this talented actor shortly afterward in a hole in the ocean floor. It was showing only two of its extremely long, thin arms and was pretending to be a poisonous sea-snake to an interested fish.

The mimic octopus lives in shallow waters off the coasts of Malaysia and Indonesia. The sandy ocean bottom in these regions offers few possibilities for hiding from enemies. So imitating predators or poisonous animals is the best way to scare the enemies off.

Since octopuses have no skeletons, these mollusks, sometimes several yards long, can slip through cracks in the rocks no more than two fingers wide when they are fleeing their enemies.

Harmless animals that imitate poisonous or predatory animals to protect themselves from being eaten are quite common in nature. But scientists know no other animal that is capable, like the mimic octopus, of impersonating several different animals.

Mimic octopuses

Since the mimic octopus can slip into other animal roles like an actor, scientists give it the sobriquet mimicus, which derives from the Latin word mimus for "actor" or "imitator."

The mimic octopus is one of the rarest octopuses in our seas. For a long time, researchers didn't even know of its existence. It was discovered only in 2001.

The only thing that the octopus, with the scientific name *Thaumoctopus mimicus*, can do with its long, thin, black-and-white-striped arms is almost magical. In a matter of seconds it can change into a flounder, a poisonous sea-snake, or, like here in this picture, into an extremely poisonous red lionfish.

Transparent and Poisonous

Have you ever stepped on a jellyfish on the beach? If so, you have surely not forgotten the painful touch of that slimy creature. Jellyfish are equipped with so-called nettle capsules at the ends of long tentacles. These capsules open at the slightest touch; then, they shoot a sort of harpoon that contains a paralyzing poison and inject it into the skin. Although it is actually intended to render prey or enemy harmless, the poison burns like fire in our skins too! The tricky thing about jellyfish is that you can hardly see them on the beach, because most of them are almost completely transparent—which is a perfect camouflage strategy for the gelatinous jellyfish.

Jellyfish have neither eyes nor ears; they only have a mouth and long arms—their tentacles—to catch prey with. They can barely move under their own power. Mostly they just let themselves be pushed around in enormous swarms by the ocean's currents.

The longest tentacles belong to a kind of jellyfish that lives in tropical seas. The poisonous arms of the Portuguese man-of-war reach up to 165 feet (50 meters) down into the depths. This jellyfish catches fish with its millions of poisonous nettle capsules.

Not every jellyfish makes itself invisible with a transparent body. The crown, or coronate, jellyfish is colored bright red and is still perfectly hidden in its environment. It lives at depths of more than 3,280 feet (1,000 meters), where red-frequency light cannot penetrate. At that depth red simply appears as black.

The long tentacles are dangerous weapons with which the jellyfish can defend itself or capture its prey. When a small fish touches one of these arms, a poisonous missile immediately shoots out of the nettle capsule into the skin of the prey. Thus, the jellyfish paralyzes its prey in a matter of seconds and swallows it whole.

Off the coast of Australia live the most poisonous jellyfish on earth. Sea wasps' tentacles, up to 10 feet (3 meters) long, hold so much poison that one of these animals alone could kill 200 humans.

Jellyfish

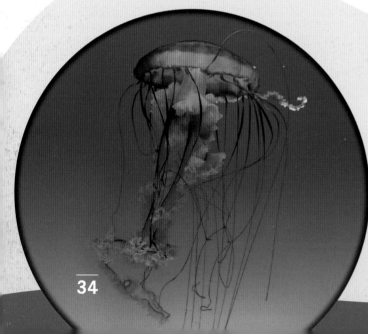

The Cassiopeia jellyfish that lives among mangrove swamps has developed an especially refined technique for eating its prey. Lying comfortably on its back on the bottom of the ocean or among corals, it swirls plankton swimming in the seawater through little openings in its body with the help of tiny cilia.

Simple, beautiful, and still unique: This *Aequorea victoria*'s body is composed of 98 percent water, which makes the animal invisible in the surrounding water. A special feature of this stringy-tentacled jellyfish is that it has illumination dots all around the edges of its bell-shaped body, which fluoresce blue or green when they are stimulated.

Invisible Hunters on the Ocean Floor

Rays are among the most elegant swimmers in the ocean. They propel themselves with their pectoral fins, which they move like waves and which look like the wings of a giant bird. It is a spectacular sight when their flat bodies glide majestically through the vastness of the ocean. When these relatives of sharks go hunting along the ocean floor, though, they make themselves as invisible as they possibly can. At a depth of no more than 65 feet (20 meters) they dig themselves into the sand so that only their eyes are visible. They wait patiently in this position for passing crabs, fish, mussels, or snails. As soon as their prey is near enough, they strike as quickly as lightning.

Many kinds of rays have notably long tails, with a stinger that they can drive painfully into other animals. The stingray's tail is even equipped with poisonous spikes, which can be used to deadly effect on humans.

Rays

Most rays' young are not born in the egg, as is usual among most fish; rather, they slip out of the egg while they are still inside the mother's body. So, the mother gives live birth to her young.

The largest rays are the mantas. Their pectoral fins can reach a span of 23 feet (7 meters). Unlike most of their relatives, the harmless mantas live, like the blue whale, on plankton, which they steer into their mouth with two extensions of their heads and then filter from the water with their gills.

Rays, which are up to 8 feet 3 inches (2 ½ meters) long, live throughout all the warmer seas. Some kinds also live in the Gulf of Mexico.

The majestic rays are inhabitants of shallow waters. They live in depths of up to 65 feet (20 meters). They like best to glide on their enormous pectoral fins just above the ocean floor.

A ray waiting in ambush: Its sand-colored skin with brown flecks lets it melt right into the sea floor. Only the eyes and breathing holes can be seen, since they are on the top of its body. Perfect camouflage. Most prey discover the bandit when it's already too late.

Well Camouflaged in Ambush

It is not hard to figure out where the seahorse gets its name. Its head looks like a horse's head, even if the rest of its body has nothing in common with the hoofed creature. In spite of their upright posture, seahorses are fish. They use their tails as grabbers to hold onto seaweeds or corals so they won't be swept away by the current. When they do lose their grip, their little dorsal fins serve as rudders. That makes their forward progress relatively slow. Seahorses are typical ambushers. They wait in their hiding places without moving until their prey swims right in front of their mouths, and then they strike fast, suck the animal in, and swallow it.

Dwarf seahorses

Seahorses are prey to only a few predators. Because of their appearance as they float among plants or corals, predator fish don't recognize them as prey. Besides, their hard outer armor, made up of bony plates, spoils most fishes' appetites.

The dwarf seahorse is the second-smallest known seahorse, after the Denise's pygmy seahorse. This midget, only ¾-inch (2 centimeters) long, lives among the coral reefs of the western Pacific.

Rearing the young seahorses is mostly up to the males. After the female has laid her eggs in the male's stomach pouch and he has fertilized them, the male incubates the eggs and later cares for the young.

When a seahorse loses a fin in a fight with one of its few predators, the fin grows back within two weeks.

Seahorses are extremely loyal animals. These ocean-dwellers need a lot of love and remain with the same partner all their lives. If one of them dies, the other one grieves a long time before finding a new partner. But usually the survivor does not live long either.

Can you find the seahorse among the thickly interwoven arms of the Gorgon reef? Only its black eyes betray the little fish. Thanks to its light gray body and its red, nipple-shaped tubercles, this cute ocean-dweller blends almost completely into its environment.

Stone or Not Stone?

Patience is half of life, the stonefish thinks. Calm as can be, it lurks for days, sometimes weeks, at the same place on the ocean floor or on a coral reef, waiting for its prey. It has made itself invisible to any victim that swims by. Its red-orange or yellow-brown skin is flecked or encrusted like a stone and strewn with all sorts of fringed outgrowths that look like algae. The stonefish digs itself down into the sand a little bit, and its perfect camouflage is done—it looks so much like a stone that it can be mistaken for one, and it's indistinguishable from the ground it lies on. Fish or crabs have no chance of recognizing this predator in ambush before it's too late; the fish opens its mouth in the blink of an eye and swallows them.

Stonefish

Careful, don't step on one! The stonefish is among the most poisonous fish on earth. The poison in the spines of its fins is so strong that it is dangerous even to humans and can be fatal. Swimmers who step on the fish thinking it's a stone are in special danger.

Stonefish live in the tropical parts of the Indian and Pacific Oceans, particularly along the Australian and South African coasts.

Like the monkfish, the stonefish is a poor swimmer; it leaves its hunting lair only reluctantly.

The stonefish, up to 15 1/5 inches (40 centimeters) long, can swallow prey as big as itself.

The stonefish wins no beauty contests with its warty skin, shaggy outgrowths, and upward-facing jaw. But this ambush-predator doesn't care a bit about its looks, as long as it is successful in its hunting!

Can you recognize the eyes and the u-shaped mouth of a stonefish here? The crusty, warty body of this bandit matches the colors and patterns of the ocean floor perfectly; it can hardly be told apart from a stone—thus its name.

Devilish Tricksters

You may know the monkfish, or sea devil, as a tasty food fish. But did you know that this thieving ocean dweller is one of the most callous tricksters in the animal kingdom? When the monkfish goes hunting, it relies completely on its magnificent camouflage. Its scale-less skin matches the ocean floor perfectly. Little shreds of skin on its body, which move in the current, look like algae or corals and let the predator's outline blur into the background. As soon as the monkfish has made itself invisible, it begins its deceptive game: it wiggles a kind of fishing pole directly in front of its mouth and cold-bloodedly lures its prey into the trap.

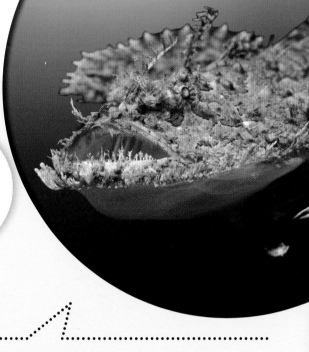

Anglerfish or monkfish

What happens when a hungry fish unknowingly bites off the lure? Never fear, the vital fold of skin grows back.

Anglerfish are pretty bad swimmers! They spend most of their life resting on the sea floor, waiting for an appetizing bit of prey to swim past.

Among the deep-sea anglerfish, only the females hunt. The males, only an inch or so long, hang on the backs of the females, who grow to as long as a 3 feet (1 meter). Over time, these little freeloaders lose even their teeth and their intestines.

Where does this "fishing pole" come from? The foremost bone of the back fin on an anglerfish—the monkfish is one type of anglerfish—grows out long like a rod. A little fold of skin at its end wiggles like a tasty morsel in front of the prey.

It takes an anglerfish only 6 milliseconds to tear open its mouth and swallow its prey. That is faster than it takes an airbag to inflate!

Look out, it's a trap! This sea devil lies on the ocean floor, almost invisible. Prey fish see only the rod with the worm-like morsel of skin, which they mistake for a wiggly treat. As soon as they go after it, the monkfish opens its huge mouth lightning-fast. That creates a suction that pulls the unsuspecting prey down the bandit's gullet.

Relatives of monkfish are the deep-sea angler-fish. They, too, lure their prey with a fishing rod. But since it is completely dark at 3,280 feet (1,000 meters) or more deep, the fold of skin that serves as bait contains an organ that lights up, luring hungry or curious fish.

Safely Hidden Dressed in Rags

As the leafy sea dragon swims through a forest of algae, you would have to look very carefully to see it at all. The folds of skin that hang from every part of its body look deceptively like brown algae. This relative of the seahorse could not hide itself any better from its enemies. But its camouflage is also useful on the hunt for small crabs and shrimp. Still, the leafy sea dragon is no swift hunter, but rather more of a slow fellow. Mostly it stays among the algae. And when it moves, it does so very, very slowly. But that, too, is part of its camouflage. That way it looks just like the algae that move with the currents.

Leafy sea dragons

Leafy sea dragons live in the warm waters off the south coast of Australia, from 10 to 165 feet (3 to 50 meters) deep.

The sea dragon does not use its funny "rags" to propel itself. For that it has inconspicuous pectoral and dorsal fins. It steers and changes direction with small fins on its head. When the sea dragon does move, it's at a speed of less than 0.62 miles (1 kilometer) per hour.

Leafy sea dragons have no teeth with which to catch or chew their prey. They simply suck fish eggs, small crabs, and shrimp through their tube-like snouts.

Like their relatives the seahorses, the sea dragon males are the ones who incubate the eggs. The female lays around 250 eggs on the male's tail, where they are fertilized, and after about eight weeks the offspring hatch. After only two days the little sea dragons go on the hunt after tiny copepod plankton and rotifers by themselves.

The sea dragon looks like a little dragon when it stretches out its leaf-like folds of skin. That's where it gets its name.

Leafy sea dragon, where are you? This sea dweller, which grows as long as 13 ½ inches (35 centimeters), relies not only on its camouflage suit of rags; its body colors also perfectly match the colors of its environment, ranging from greenish-yellow to brownish-red.

Hocus Pocus, See Right Through Me!

Fish that live in large schools normally find it difficult to protect themselves from predators. Since they live mostly in open waters without plant growth and thus have no cover, they can't hide or mislead their enemies with tricks like having bodies the same color as the sea floor or mock growths of seaweed. For some of these fish, nature has invented something special in the way of camouflage: their bodies are diaphanous and appear, in the shimmering underwater light, simply transparent.

Diaphanous bodies as a camouflage strategy are quite common in the animal kingdom. The larvae of many fish, like the paperfish, are protected by an almost transparent body.

Glass catfish

The Indian glass catfish has a smaller relative, the ghost catfish, which is only about 3 inches (8 centimeters) long. It is known as a ghost catfish because it is transparent like a ghost.

It's almost unbelievable, but even in the deepest ocean, fish camouflage themselves with diaphanous bodies. They protect themselves in this way from predators who go hunting with light-producing organs.

The characteristic of bodies that allows light to pass through them is called translucence, a word that compounds the Latin words trans for "through" and lux for "light."

Its translucent body keeps the Indian glass catfish from casting a silhouette against the light, and from drawing the attention of its predators to its dark spot. Instead, its body always takes on the colors of its background. The shining green of algae simply shimmers right through it.

The glass catfish's body is transparent right down to the bones and the inner organs, which are directly behind its head.

In the bright flash of an undersea camera the bodies of these Indian glass catfish are easy to recognize. But in the normal half-darkness underwater, these freshwater natives of Southeast Asia are practically invisible.

The King of the Frogs and His Clothing

When you hear croaking from your neighbor's garden pond, it is generally not from a tree frog but from one of the widespread varieties of pond or water frogs. True, the tree frog, about 1 ½ inches (4 centimeters) long, is the best known kind of frog in the northern latitudes, but it's very hard to catch a glimpse of it. In contrast to its relatives, the pond frogs, this bright green frog spends most of the daylight hours on trees or bushes! It seeks water only while hunting at night or during its spawning period. So it's a good thing the cute little hoppers are so perfectly color-coordinated for life among bark and leaves: their skin color changes according to the background—from shiny green to brown to mouse gray—and can even have multicolored spots.

Tree frogs

It's very rare but you may even find a bright blue tree frog. Such a frog is missing the yellow pigment in its skin to mix with the blue and make green.

Did you know that frogs don't drink? They absorb the liquid they need through their skins.

The loudest croakers in our latitudes are the tree frogs. That is because the male can inflate his vocal sac at the front of his throat to almost the size of his body when he croaks. On a quiet summer night you can hear a frog choir's rhythmic erpp, erpp, erpp at a distance of up to 1 ¼ miles (2 kilometers).

Tree frogs cannot, like the Frog King in the fairy tale, turn into a handsome prince; still, they can quickly change their appearance. For example, they adopt a brown coloring when they are climbing up a tree trunk. And even during winter hibernation, which these animals spend underground, they camouflage themselves in brown.

Tree frogs are the only frog species native to us that can climb up tree trunks and branches. They do that with the aid of suction cups on their toes. For these acrobatic climbers, not even smooth surfaces like plates of glass are a problem.

It seems this insect could not hold still! Once the tree frog spots its movement, there is no escape. Quick as a flash the green jumper leaps forward, shoots out its sticky tongue, and hauls the helpless prey into its mouth.

The tree frog as everyone knows it: The tiny hopper shimmers bright green when it's sitting on a leaf or among the grass. Many glands in the frog's skin secrete a slimy liquid to keep the frog from dehydrating. That is what makes it look so shiny.

Upside Down and Dressed as Bark

The leaf-tailed gecko spends its days pressed up against the trunk of a tree, flat as a flounder, before it goes off on the hunt for insects as darkness descends. While these lizards, nearly 7 ¾ inches (20 centimeters) long, rest, they make themselves almost invisible. Like other geckos, they can cleverly match their skin color to their background. However, the change in skin color from gray-green to greenish-gray to black is hardly all they can do! The leaf-tailed geckos have some quite different tricks in their repertoire!

Leaf-tailed geckos

How did geckos get their name? These reptiles got it from the reputation of a kind of gecko that lives in Indonesia called the tokeh. It calls out in a loud and clear voice, "Tokeh" or "Gecko."

Geckos live inside houses in many tropical countries, as houseflies do in ours. They perch on the walls and scurry across the ceilings hunting for insects.

Comfortable, Mr. Leaf-tailed Gecko? This little lizard hangs upside-down on the tree trunk during the day. Its large eyes, with their slit-shaped pupils, mark the gecko as a night hunter; the slit gathers the light rays so well that the leaf-tailed gecko has very keen night vision.

The leaf-tailed gecko lives only on the island of Madagascar in the Indian Ocean, off the east coast of Africa. When animals or plants live in only one single region of the world, scientists call them "endemic."

Why can geckos climb up smooth walls and even panes of glass? The secret is in their feet. Super-fine bristles grow on their broad toes. Weak electrical currents arise between them and the surface, which attract each other and are strong enough to hold these light-weight reptiles to the wall.

The camouflage trick with the tree-bark costume: The leaf-tailed gecko's body is covered with small crusty spots that look like the lichen or moss that grows on the tree's bark. Its flat tail, which looks like a leaf and gives the leaf-tailed gecko its name, and little flaps of skin lie flat on the bark and blur the outlines of the lizard's body.

Colorful, More Colorful, Chameleon

Chameleons are the most unique lizards in the world. With high backs, oblate bodies, bulging eyes, and long tails they can use to grab onto branches, these reptiles look really primeval. Chameleons' ability to change colors is legendary. But did you know that the chameleon changes color mostly to express its mood? The color changes serve primarily as camouflage for only a few types, like the dwarf chameleons of the species *Bradypodion*.

How does the chameleon change colors? In its skin it has color cells in several layers one on top of the other. In the uppermost layer are the cells for yellow and red; the second layer holds those for the brown and black shades; and in the bottom layer are the cells that reflect sunlight and look blue. According to whichever layers are active at any moment, the lizard's body mixes its color.

Chameleons

Chameleons can move their eyes independently. That has incalculable advantages for hunting. Without turning its head, the chameleon can follow the movements of a fly or a beetle until the victim is in exactly the right place. Then the long tongue comes out unerringly to catch its prey.

Did you know that chameleons cannot control their changes in color consciously? Nerve stimuli are responsible for a chameleon being a shimmering green in one moment and a second later it's spotted red and black.

The chameleon's tongue is longer than its entire body, including the tail. Its prey gets stuck on the gluey tip of the tongue and gets swallowed whole.

"I'd like to have babies with you." "No, thank you." That's how the "color conversation" between these two carpet chameleons might be translated into our language. Most chameleons change color in order to communicate with their fellow species members. They also indicate the threat of danger, their own fear, or hunger by changing color.

Compared to its relatives, who like to show off their bright colors, the flap-necked chameleon prefers muted shades. As a consequence, it is perfectly camouflaged. Its green-spotted skin with its bright sprinkles looks like sunlight through leaves. Under stress, or when it's angry or anxious, it shows a conspicuous pattern of black spots as well as a stripe from its shoulder to the middle of its body.

Lizard in a Spiky Outfit

Predators think twice about whether they ought to take a bite out of the thorny devil lizard, because an animal might not necessarily want to make the acquaintance of the sharp thorns the thorny devil has all over its body, legs, and tail, or with the two pointy growths above its eyes and on its neck. The thorny devil (sometimes called the desert devil) grows to about 7 ¾ inches (20 centimeters) and lives in the hot dry deserts and steppes of Australia. Even though they look so frightening, these little lizards are completely harmless ant eaters—another reason for them to go for an absolutely surefire camouflage.

Thorny devils

The thorny devil looks dangerous in its suit of spikes. Still, the harmless lizard nourishes itself only on ants and termites. The reptile devours around 2,000 of these crawlers for each meal.

If you've got such a scary outside, surely you'll have no friends. Far from it! Actually, the thorny devil is a very social animal. The night-hunting ant eater likes to meet its fellow lizards for a nice sun bath during the day.

Why are the thorny devil's legs so long? So it doesn't burn its belly on the red-hot desert floor.

Why does the thorny devil sometimes pick its legs up high? Has the ground under its feet suddenly become too hot? No, it is scared stiff. When danger threatens, the thorny devil stiffens for a moment in its movement—even when it has just lifted up its leg to walk.

The thorny devil doesn't need to drink. The rare raindrop is enough for it, or the drops of dew that condense on its body overnight and trickle down to its mouth through tiny furrows.

This thorny devil poses for the camera, armed from head to toe. The spiky ant eater relies not only on its suit of spikes, however, to frighten off its predators. With its beige-brownish skin color it is scarcely noticeable on the desert floor. Its spiky exterior also reminds an observer's passing glance more of a dry leaf or a piece of thorn bush. So it tricks the hungry hunters into thinking it is completely inedible.

Shy Prairie Rattlers

There's hardly a western movie out there without the excited maraca sound of rattlesnakes in the background as cowboys and Indians ride across the prairie. Rattlesnakes, between 6 ½ to 8 ¼ feet (2 to 2 ½ meters) long, are native to America and are among the most poisonous snakes on earth. They use their poison not only to stun and kill their prey, but also as an effective defense. When they feel threatened, they first shake the rattles at the end of their tails. If that doesn't dissuade the attacker they shoot their head forward, quick as a flash, and bite. Although a poisoned bite from a rattlesnake is often fatal to animals and humans, these snakes would rather rely on their camouflage than on their dangerous poisonous fangs.

Rattlesnakes

"Attention, this is your last warning! Do not come any closer!" is what the rattlesnake is saying with this attack position. Its challenge is clear and emphatic—it's coiled, ready to strike, and its tail is rattling. Whoever does not do as it says will make the acquaintance of its poisonous fangs.

These stealthy hunters are well-hidden as they sneak up on their prey. If a rat, rabbit, or a prairie dog comes too close, the rattlesnake shoots forward like lightning and bites with its poisonous fangs. The dead prey is then swallowed whole.

Rattlesnakes bear live young. Instead of being enclosed in a hard eggshell, the offspring are wrapped in a thin membrane that is slipped off shortly after they are born.

Each of the twenty-nine different kinds of rattlesnakes living in America has its own poison cocktail. Some poisons destroy the blood vessel walls and simultaneously hinder the blood's coagulation, so that the prey bleeds to death internally. Other poisons paralyze or suffocate the victim.

The rattle at the end of the snake's tail is composed of several rings of horny scales. When snakes grow, they shed their skins. Rattlesnakes, however, do not discard the horny scales at the ends of their tails. These leftovers of dry skin are what make up the rattle.

Rattlesnakes spend the days mostly well hidden in the brush or in hollows and clefts of rocks. The diamond pattern of their yellowish, brown, red, or black skin help them to remain perfectly camouflaged on the dry desert floor or on the prairie.

Fluorescent Green and Still Invisible

When you see a tree snake, a green adder, or a green mamba for the first time, you'd think these snakes would catch anyone's eye. Their fluorescent light-green scaly skin is utterly conspicuous to any observer. Hard to believe, then, that this attention-grabbing color actually works as the snakes' camouflage. That's because these animals live mainly on rainforest trees in the tropical regions of Africa and Asia. And what color is the least visible among a perpetually green thicket of leaves? Why, green, of course!

Green tree snakes

The harmless relative: The spotted bush snake is a native of Africa and grows to only 4 feet (1 $\frac{1}{5}$ meters) long. Among the thick foliage of tropical forests this non-poisonous adder is perfectly camouflaged on its hunt for lizards or tree frogs.

The mamba's big eyes with round pupils, as well as their two harmless relatives in the adder family, betray the fact that these snakes hunt by day. Snakes that are active primarily at night or in the dim light of dusk, like the rattlesnake, have only thin slits for pupils.

Green mambas are much feared by humans, on account of their very dangerous poison and their aggressiveness. The diurnal poisonous adder prefers to hunt in bushes and trees, but can also often be seen on the ground.

Have you ever noticed a snake flicking its tongue in and out? It does that in order to "taste" its surroundings. When the snakes stretch out their tongues, tiny aromatic particles stick to it. Back inside its mouth, the tongue, with its bits of fragrance, is folded against the snake's gums, the so-called vomeronasal or Jacobson's organ, where sensory cells pick up the bits of aroma.

Mambas, which grow as long as 13 feet (4 meters), are regarded as the fastest snakes on earth. On the ground they can move at speeds of up to 15 miles (24 kilometers) per hour. To escape a poisonous mamba, you'd have to run as fast as a one-hundred meter sprinter.

Birds, lizards, frogs, and small mammals are the tasty treats the mamba in its tree is waiting for. It glides soundlessly from branch to branch to get closer to its victims. Usually the prey notices—too late—the bright green body with the large scales among the perpetually green trees of the rainforest.

Like a Stick in the Reeds

The bittern is a master of invisibility! This member of the heron family, up to 2 ½ feet (80 centimeters) tall with a thick body and short neck, lives in tall reeds on the edges of swamps, moorlands, ponds, and lakes. When the bittern feels threatened, it stretches its neck, head, and beak straight up and freezes in that position. That way its yellowish-brown striped feathers with light and dark spots that look like reflections of sunlight blend into the surrounding reeds, and the bird's outline is completely lost among the reed stems. It's a perfect camouflage, which protects the bittern and its brood from predators.

Bitterns

Because of the hollow booming sound of the male's mating call, the bittern's name ultimately drives from two Latin words, butio for "bittern" and taurus for "bull" or "cow." This is most easily seen in the bittern's French name, butor, and in German it is often called a "moorcow."

You are more likely to hear a bittern than see one. The males, seeking receptive females, send out their calls from February to June. The mating call can be heard up to 3 miles (5 kilometers) away and sounds like someone blowing over the top of an empty bottle.

Bitterns build their nests among the reeds. Their young are well camouflaged with their brown fuzzy feathers. A week after they hatch from the egg they already instinctively take the stick-in-the-reeds position when danger is near.

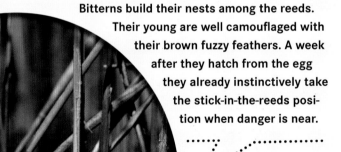

Bitterns live near water and need broad expanses of reeds in order to hide themselves. These herons feel especially at home by a pond with thick growths of reed around it, or in moors and swamps.

Do you recognize the bittern among the reeds? It is very well camouflaged among the dry reed stems, with its yellowish-brown striped feathers. To hide even better, it uses a simple trick: it sways its body gently back and forth the way reeds do in the wind.

Invisible—Looks Like Bark

Do you know the tawny owl's call? *Who whoohoohoo whooo* it calls all through the night near forests, parks, or gardens with lots of old trees. Night scenes in horror movies often feature this sound to heighten the tension onscreen. But can you see the tawny owl? Only very rarely, for this raptor, about 15 ½ inches (40 centimeters) tall, is active only as dusk falls and goes hunting for mice and birds after dark. But during the day you'd have to be very alert to discover the tawny owl, because it sits hidden in trees—its feathers the same color as tree bark—and dozes with half-closed eyes.

Tawny owls

Tawny owls are, like all their relatives of the owl family, soundless hunters. Hunting for mice, they often glide softly through the air on their great wings, and when the slightest rustle or squeak betrays a mouse's presence, they drop down on their prey.

The tawny owl devours mice and small birds whole. After the prey has been digested, the owl vomits up the indigestible bones, feathers, and fur, the so-called "cast."

Like its fellow owls, the tawny owl has a "facial disc." These specially shaped feathers that frame its face don't serve the owl as a fashion statement; rather, they help catch additional sound waves and guide them to the owl's ears, thus amplifying its hearing.

The tawny owl cannot move its coal black eyes. When it wants to look in a different direction, it has to turn its whole head. But it does that masterfully: This bird easily turns its head through a three-quarters circle (270 degrees). We humans can turn just a quarter of a circle.

Tree or owl? You need sharp eyes to see the tawny owl on a tree by day. The brown and white stripes along its feathers blend completely with the tree's bark. White flecks on its wings imitate spots of sunlight in a bright forest and complete a perfect camouflage.

Tawny owls love big old trees, where they rest through the day. If they do not find their prey by gliding through the air, they often sit on branches and wait until they espy their intended victims on the forest floor with their excellent ears and sharp eyes. Then, they plummet down on their prey.

Can you see us? The feathers of even the youngest tawny owls already have the typical bark color. So they are safe as they sit on an old tree trunk and wait for their mother to come back from the hunt.

Carnival in the Rainforest

Parrots are probably the most brightly-colored birds in nature. It's hard to believe that they wear their colorful feather-clothes not so that they'll be noticed, but so they can hide! You can barely see a green macaw among the thick foliage of the South American rainforests. Multi-colored iridescent lories look like brightly blooming bushes, and even the Brazilian hyacinthine macaw, the largest parrot at up to a 3 feet (1 meter) long, makes itself invisible among the shadows of the rainforest with its dark blue plumage.

Parrots

Parrots are "three-legged" climbers. They use not only their talons, two claws facing front and two facing back on each foot, but also their beaks to climb skillfully among the branches or on steep cliff walls.

Parrots can live to a dignified old age. The cockatoos live longest, up to 75 years in domesticity.

Gray parrots are excellent voice imitators. All day long they chatter back what they hear from their owners, the radio, or the TV.

Parrots are social birds. They often travel in swarms of up to a thousand birds.

With their powerful, downward-curving beaks, macaws can even crack open the hard shells of Brazil nuts; we need a strong pair of nutcrackers to do this!

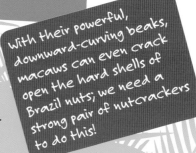

Did you know that there are right- and left-footed parrots? They hold nuts and fruits with their favored foot as they eat, unless the tasty foodstuffs are growing right in front of their beaks.

This green-feathered parrot is barely visible among the long palm leaves. Other parrots are not so reserved in their choice of plumage. They decorate themselves with vibrant red, green, yellow, and blue feathers.

Longears with White Vests

Mountain hares love the cold! In the high peaks of the Alps, in cold Scandinavia, Siberia, North America, and even icy Greenland they feel right at home. They are so crazy about life in the cold—with an abundance of snowfall—that they dress themselves in white fur during the coldest times of the year. If they were to have normal, gray-brown rabbit fur, their enemies like snowy owls, lynxes, and arctic foxes would find the mountain hares far too easily on the sparkling white snow. But with his white fur, Mr. Longears is perfectly camouflaged as he squats in a snow hollow to avoid danger. In springtime, when the snow melts, the mountain hare puts on its gray-brown coat again. Clever, huh?

Mountain hares

The colder the climate where the mountain hare lives, the shorter its ears are! It is through the ears that the mountain hare loses body warmth to the surrounding environment and thus regulates its body temperature. The longer the ears, the more warmth it loses!

There are other animals that camouflage themselves with white fur in places where there is a lot of snow; for example, the arctic fox and the stoat (the ermine). The snow grouse and the snowy owl grow white feathers as well.

The mountain hares that live in Scotland and Ireland demonstrate how well this animal has adapted to its environment. Since it snows very seldom in those places, the mountain hares do not color themselves white in winter. On the other hand, mountain hares that live on the year-round ice of the Arctic always wear white.

Mountain hares, like their relatives the brown hares, are active at dusk and night. During the days they squat in snow or earthen hollows.

Look out—danger from the rear! *Better get out of here*, thinks the brown hare. Its gray-brown fur, which works fine as camouflage in the forest, moorland, or tundra, is unfortunately useless on snow-covered fields!

In the winter, the black tips of the mountain hare's ears are the only thing that betrays its presence. The rest of its fur can barely be distinguished from the snow-covered landscape.

For the mountain hare, its white coat is a matter of life and death, for it has no cover where it can seek safe haven in case of danger. Instead, it flattens itself against the ground and makes itself as invisible as possible.

White on the Permanent Ice

White harp seal babies look indescribably cuddly. Their white coats, however, are not only beautiful, but also are ideal camouflage. Young harp seals, you see, have neither nest nor cave where they can hide. They lie on the ice, unprotected, when their mothers go hunting for fish in the northern polar seas. But their white fur helps the youngsters melt into their surroundings and makes them very difficult for their worst enemies, the polar bears, to see. The polar bears also use the white fur trick. But they do it so they can sneak up on their prey better!

Harp seals

Harp seals get their name from the horseshoe-shaped spot the adults have on their backs, which looks like a kind of harp.

Seals are not born knowing how to swim. After they've spent their first few weeks on the ice, they must learn how to swim, dive, and hunt.

Before the pups move from the ice into the water at the age of a few weeks, they exchange their white baby fluff for an adult's gray-black fur with a light-colored belly.

Harp seals hunt the ocean for fish and crabs. In doing so, these mammals sometimes dive hundreds of yards down into the sea and remain underwater for up to half an hour.

A kiss for mama! Harp seal mothers suckle their pups for only ten to twelve days. Their milk is so full of fat that the pups gain weight at a rate of up to 4 ½ pounds (2 kilograms) a day.

Harp seals live in the arctic waters near the pack ice and spend most of their lives in the water. They come onto the land only in spring in order to give birth to their young.

Three black spots are all you can see of this harp seal. From a distance you can hardly make out the white fur balls on the snow. And harp seals don't mind lying on the ice at all! A dense fur coat and a thick layer of fat protect them from the cold.

Silent Hunters

When the leopard is on the hunt, not the least rustle or cracking branch can be heard. This silent hunter creeps along, crouching close to the ground and shielded by the high grasses of the African plains, completely unnoticed even within a few yards of its prey—usually an antelope, zebra, or warthog. Then it lies motionless for minutes, observing its victim, which has no idea it is about to be attacked. At the right moment the leopard suddenly springs forward with a powerful leap and kills its prey with one bite to the throat.

Leopards

Leopards are extraordinarily strong animals. They drag an antelope, which weighs more than they do, effortlessly up among the branches of a tree, where it will be safe from jealous food rivals.

The South American jaguar is related to the African and Asiatic leopards. The only visible difference is a small black mark inside the jaguar's spots.

Sprinting leopards do not have the endurance of the super-fast cheetahs. But they don't need it. Once the well-camouflaged creatures have crept up close enough to their victims, they can leap more than 33 feet (10 meters) from a still position onto their clueless prey.

Black panthers are also leopards. A particular gene gives them their black fur. Even normally colored leopard parents can have a black cub among their litter. Black panthers are found frequently in Malaysia and the high mountains of Ethiopia.

This big cat, native to the African and Asian tropics, frequently lurks in trees, waiting for prey. It either drops down on its victims from the branches or runs cleverly down, hiding behind the trunk of the tree, to attack at the best moment.

Prey can barely see the leopard, with its luminous yellow fur flecked with black spots, among the dry grasses of the arid plains and savannas.

Leopards, with their flexible bodies, elegant movement, and distinctive markings on their fur, are among the most beautiful of the big cats.

Living on the Hot Desert Sands

As dusk falls over the Sahara Desert and the temperature becomes somewhat cooler, the desert fox creeps out of its underground home and goes hunting. Mice, lizards, grasshoppers, and insects are among its favorite foods. The fennec, as the desert fox is also called, pinpoints every tiny sound with its huge ears. This hunter, about the size of a rabbit, has a sand-colored coat that provides good camouflage—and also protects it from its main enemy, the African or Persian lynx. In case of danger, the desert fox can bury itself within seconds in the loose desert sand. Invisible to any attacker!

Desert foxes

The desert fox lives in one of the driest and hottest places on earth. Temperatures up to 140 degrees Fahrenheit (60 degrees Celsius) and sometimes not a drop of rain for years make the North African Sahara a most inhospitable living environment.

Desert fox, why do you have such big ears? The better to keep me cool! The ears, which are up to 4 inches (10 centimeters) long, as big as its whole head, protect the desert fox from overheating. The ears allow excess heat to flow away from the fox's body, because desert foxes cannot sweat.

Desert foxes do not need to drink. The water carried by their prey—in their blood, for example—is enough for desert foxes to survive on.

Desert foxes don't even pant in the heat the way their relatives, the dogs, do. Panting would make them lose far too much moisture. And that is precious stuff in the desert!

Thick fur pads under the desert fox's paws protect it from the burning hot desert sand. But the pads also help it to get sure footing on the loose ground.

72

A sand-colored desert fox on sandy ground. The fox's light-colored fur offers not only great camouflage, but also protects the animal from becoming too hot.

A desert fox mother with a fluffy whelp. The desert fox's fur coat is soft and very thick. How come? A thick coat keeps out not only the cold at night but also the heat, and thereby protects the desert fox from overheating.

Through the Branches in Slow Motion

Hardly any animal is more sluggish than the sloth. This cute relative of the anteater spends its entire life in the trees of the South and Central American tropical rainforests, and moves at a speed of 6 ½ feet (2 meters) per minute—when it moves at all. It sleeps for more than half the day, hanging upside down from the branches. The animal's laziness, however, is a trick of nature: marauding predators like raptors, jaguars, or boa constrictors become aware of their prey when it moves. They don't even notice the infinitely slow movements of the sloth. Lucky sloth!

Sloths

Why move at all, when leaves grow right into your mouth? **thinks the sloth. It's much lovelier just to dangle from a branch and doze. But this leisurely lifestyle is a survival tactic: By using as little energy as possible, the sloth can live solely on the nutrient-poor leaves it finds in the tree crowns.**

Once a week the sloths leave their homes among the branches to come down to earth and use the bathroom. In order not to give themselves away they bury their business carefully in a small hole in the ground. That can take as long as half an hour!

The sloth's claws, up to 2 ¾ inches (7 centimeters) long, not only serve as climbing aids and let the animal hang onto branches, but, if a sloth is attacked, it can give its enemy deep wounds with these sharp tools.

It's hard to believe, but sloths are good swimmers!

Sloths can be recognized by the number of their toes and fingers. All sloths have, instead of the usual mammalian five toes on their hind feet, only three. There are two types of sloths: two-toed, with two fingers on their front feet, and three-toed, with three.

Sloths are nature's energy-savers: their body temperature is much lower than other mammals'. When they're asleep it can drop as low as 50 degrees Fahrenheit (10 degrees Celsius). Their metabolism is also only half as fast, and because they sleep so much and move so slowly, their bodies are almost always at rest.

Sloths are so slow that algae grow in their shaggy fur. Their otherwise brown fur coat then looks quite green, which guarantees them an almost 100 percent complete camouflage among the thick leaves and branches of the tropical rainforest!

Sloths spend practically their entire lives in trees. They hook themselves onto a branch or tree trunk with their long claws and eat, sleep, and procreate in this position.

Well Protected by White Spots

Roe deer are terrible mothers. When they give birth to their fawns in May or June, they simply deposit them in the high grass or under a bush at the edge of the forest and come back only to suckle the little ones. But what seems like cruel neglect at first sight is actually a survival strategy: the fawns' red-brown coat with white spots makes them practically invisible in the high grass or bush to foxes and lynx—their predators. And nature has invented another trick for the roes: fawns have no odor and their whereabouts can therefore not be sniffed out by their enemies. If the mothers were to remain in the area, though, they would immediately draw the enemies' attention to themselves and their defenseless young.

Roe deer

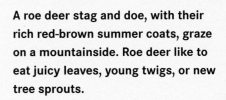

A roe deer stag and doe, with their rich red-brown summer coats, graze on a mountainside. Roe deer like to eat juicy leaves, young twigs, or new tree sprouts.

Since roe deer have no endurance when fleeing their enemies, they need high grass or undergrowth where they can hide silently when they sense danger. Thus, their brown fur offers them good camouflage.

After the fawn is born, the doe licks it until it has no smell of its own. In the daily struggle for survival, that is basic grooming!

Don't mix them up! Roe deer belong to the deer family. But real deer, like the fallow deer or the elk, are far larger than roe deer. Female deer are also not called deer but does, and the young deer are called fawns. And the male roe deer is called a stag.

If you come across a fawn in the bushes at the edge of the forest or in the high grass, you must not touch it for any reason. That would make the fawn smell of a human, and the doe would reject it.

Spots on a fur coat or dappled sunlight? The white spots on this brown fur look like spots of sunshine and thus camouflage this fawn on its bed of dry leaves perfectly. After it is born, the fawn spends three months lying curled up in the high grass or the protective brush. When danger comes near, the animal does not flee but presses itself flat against the ground.

Index

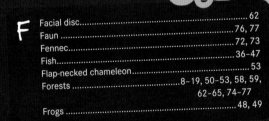

Photo Credits